CONTENTS

FROM THE EDITOR

This month, we honor and focus exclusively on women entrepreneurs.

Women entrepreneurs encounter distinct hurdles, yet enterprises led by women persist in expanding and prospering, significantly impacting both local and worldwide economies.

Kara James of both Pursue and Thrive and Strategic Advisor Board is our featured entrepreneur. She does amazing work and has a powerful story. She pursues excellence and success with a laser-like focus and serves tirelessly.

You'll also be motivated by the stories and lessons from the following powerful businesswomen:

Julia Akinyooye	Elisa Molina
Tatiana Chamorro	Corinne Morahan
Laura McCann	Nailah Queen
Sandra Jacquemin	Kim Rittberg
Jodi Klaristenfeld	Susie Schaefer
Staci Millard	

PIVOT Magazine

Founder and President
Jason Miller
jason@strategicadvisorboard.com

Editor-in-Chief
Chris O'Byrne
chris@jetlaunch.net

Design
JETLAUNCH.net

Advertising
Chris O'Byrne
chris@jetlaunch.net

Webmaster
Joel Phillips
joel@proshark.com

Editor
Laura West
laura@jetlaunch.net

Cover Design
Debbie O'Byrne

FROM THE DESK OF THE PRESIDENT

As president of PIVOT, I'd like to take this opportunity to express my support and admiration for women entrepreneurs around the world. As we celebrate International Women's Month, I'm reminded of the incredible achievements of women who have broken through glass ceilings and defied societal norms to pursue their dreams of building successful businesses.

Women entrepreneurs face unique challenges, from accessing funding to breaking through in male-dominated industries. Despite these obstacles, women-owned businesses continue to grow and thrive, making important contributions to local and global economies. Studies have shown that women-led businesses are more profitable and innovative, proving that diversity and inclusion are important factors for success in the business world.

In our magazine, we're committed to making the voices of women entrepreneurs heard by sharing their stories and insights to inspire others to pursue their own entrepreneurial ventures. We're proud to be a platform for women to showcase their talents and accomplishments.

But our work isn't done. We must continue to advocate for greater gender equality in the business world and create more opportunities for women to succeed and become leaders. This means advocating for policies and programs that support women-owned businesses, investing in women entrepreneurs, and combating gender biases and stereotypes that hold women back.

To all the women entrepreneurs out there, we see you, we hear you, and we support you. Your hard work, determination, and perseverance are an inspiration to us all. As we tackle the challenges of a changing global economy, it's women entrepreneurs who are leading the way, creating innovative solutions, and driving economic growth.

Let's celebrate the achievements of women entrepreneurs and renew our commitment to building a more inclusive and equitable business world. Let's all work together to create a future where every woman succeeds and thrives in business, no matter where she is in the world.

PURSUE AND THRIVE: HELPING COACHES AND CEOS BUILD PROFITABLE AND SUSTAINABLE BUSINESSES

KARA JAMES

In February 2018, I had a life-changing experience when I suffered severe internal bleeding because of complications from a hemicolectomy. This experience forced me to take a step back and focus on my health and recovery. During this time, I deepened my passion for coaching and learned about business strategies I had wanted to explore for years. This experience inspired me to pursue my passion for coaching, and I haven't looked back since.

As a "serial learner," I've spent the last five years devouring dozens of business strategy books and certifications, including Keap/Infusionsoft for automation; proposal writing, copywriting, and funnel building from FG Society; and productivity from HarvardX. I'm dedicated to constantly learning and growing, and I make it a point to learn at least one new strategic step for business growth every day.

With my knowledge and experience, I've helped coaches and CEOs at every stage of their business, from startup to scaling successful companies. My expertise has allowed me to help my clients develop various offerings that generate consistent income and deliver these offerings and programs in a variety of formats, including courses, evergreen programs, group coaching, and retreats.

My ideal clients for my business Pursue and Thrive are women coaches who are beyond the startup phase and need help creating or perfecting their programs. As a consultant with the Strategic Advisor Board, I help CEOs in a variety of industries with their offers. In both positions, my ideal client is also interested in hosting their own retreat.

My ideal client is someone who knows the importance of having clear direction and a solid plan to grow their business but doesn't know the best way to go about creating it. They also recognize the value of investing in their business and is committed to achieving their goals. They know that success doesn't happen overnight, and they're willing to put in the effort to achieve their vision.

My clients often feel overwhelmed by the many decisions they need to make and the uncertainty of which direction to go. They may be facing growth challenges, struggling to manage their team, or are trying to take their business in a new direction. They recognize they need support to overcome these challenges and succeed.

I help CEOs and entrepreneurs who are at a crossroads and need guidance on how to take the next steps to achieve their goals. I offer a customized approach to help my clients develop a clear strategy for their business, align their team with their vision, and overcome any obstacles that prevent them from achieving their goals. With my help, my clients can make informed decisions, gain clarity, and move forward with confidence. I work with them to create a roadmap for success that is tailored to their business and their unique circumstances.

I help coaches and business leaders gain the clarity they need to create an incredible, compelling offer or program that is unique and helps them stand out from all the noise. I pick them up where they're at. They know who they want to serve and have a good idea of how to serve them, but they need that crystal clear clarity on, not only the who, but also the how, and most importantly, the why. The why is often overlooked, yet it's the most important part because people want to know why you do what you do. This is the most important building block for the "know, like, and trust" factor, and without it, your chances for success are slim.

Together, we dig deep, and my clients are often surprised and impressed at how deep we go. They're so excited when it has clicked with them personally and their program almost writes itself. We start by building a strong business foundation that will last in this ever-changing world. Then, I teach them the more than a dozen components that make an offer absolutely irresistible, as well as another dozen key factors for a compelling sales page that appeals to customers. When they combine these two factors with a concrete business foundation, they have built a business that will generate consistent income for years to come.

My product or service is the best solution for coaches and CEOs who are new to the industry because I know exactly what it takes to make a coaching business a successful and thriving one. As someone who has been in the industry for a long time, I have a wealth of experience with helping coaches and CEOs create various offers that generate consistent income and provide these offers and programs in a variety of formats, such as courses, evergreen programs, group coaching, and retreats.

I know building a successful coaching business isn't easy, and many components must be aligned to make it work. If even one aspect isn't right, it can jeopardize the entire business. That's why I offer a comprehensive approach that covers all the important elements of a successful coaching business. This includes developing a clear brand message, identifying target clients, creating offerings that fit their needs, and pricing, marketing, and sales strategies.

With my help, coaches and CEOs build a sustainable and profitable business that provides them with a steady income stream while fulfilling their passion for helping others. My approach is unique because I tailor it to each client's individual needs, goals, and vision. I believe in creating a personalized roadmap for success for each client that includes all the components needed for their business to thrive.

Overall, my service is the best solution for coaches and CEOs who want to build a profitable coaching business that aligns with their values, passion, and vision. With my knowledge and experience, I can help them avoid the pitfalls and mistakes that new

coaches often face and help them build a thriving and successful coaching business.

As a certified business retreat planner, I also help my clients create beautiful retreats for their clients, helping them offer unique and transformative experiences while generating additional revenue for their business. I believe in a personalized approach tailored to each client's needs, goals, and vision, and I'm committed to helping them succeed in a sustainable and profitable way.

As a coach, I've helped many coaches focus on their areas of expertise and develop incredible programs perfectly tailored to their clients. One example that stands out to me is an alignment coach who came to me with a program based on the Law of Attraction and how to help others tap into everything the universe provides. However, after a few sessions together and getting to know her better, we agreed that there was an even better path for her future.

Based on her knowledge, experience, and expertise in quantum physics and her personal experiences as a young widow, we built her grief coaching business. Her unique and personalized program helps many widows navigate their own grief journey and find joy in life again. The program is tailored to each client's needs, based on where they're in their grief process, making it effective and rewarding for both the coach and the client.

I'm incredibly proud to have helped pave this path for her, and I often receive messages from her thanking me for the transformative impact we have made together—not only for her but for her clients as well. Soon, I'll be helping her create a retreat for her and her clients to have an even more personal, connecting, and deeply transformative experience.

Overall, I believe in the power of coaching to transform lives, and I help coaches create programs that are unique, effective, and tailored to their clients' needs. I'm honored to be a part of their journey and help them make a difference in the world.

Becoming a successful entrepreneur isn't easy, and it takes tenacity and perseverance to overcome the challenges that come with it. It's important to remember that failure and mistakes are a natural part of the process, and they can often serve as valuable learning experiences. As an entrepreneur myself, I've experienced many failures and setbacks, but I've never thought of giving up.

I firmly believe that the key to success is staying positive and believing in yourself, even in the face of adversity. It's important to always move forward and never lose sight of the goal. The road may be difficult, but the rewards are worth it.

I know that my success as an entrepreneur results from my perseverance and unwavering commitment to my goals. I've fallen down many times, but I've always gotten back up and kept going. I trust in my abilities and my vision for my business and never take a single moment for granted.

In summary, becoming a successful entrepreneur takes hard work, dedication, and a willingness to learn from mistakes and setbacks. It's important to stay positive, believe in yourself, and always keep going, even when things get tough. With the right attitude and approach, anyone can achieve their goals and succeed in the world of entrepreneurship.

To learn more about my advisory role with the Strategic Advisor Board, coaching programs, including upcoming retreats, and my newest program launching this spring, "Experiences on Evergreen," a comprehensive program designed to help coaches and CEOs take their business to the next by selling their high-ticket programs and offers on autopilot, visit pursueandthrive.com, https://linktr.ee/karajamesbizcoach, and strategicadvisorboard.com

Reach out by booking a call at https://rebrand.ly/pursueandthrivecall or by sending an email to karajames@pursueandthrive.com or kara@strategicadvisorboard.com.

HOW INDEPENDENT PUBLISHING CAN BENEFIT YOUR BUSINESS

SUSIE SCHAEFER

My ideal client is a seasoned executive, CEO, coach, consultant, or entrepreneur who has a deep connection to their "why" I like to work with people who have built their business around a mission and are connected to the community through the products or services they provide. These are usually people who have a desire to positively impact others and serve humanity profoundly.

Most of my clients want to expand their reach and understand that a book is a great marketing tool. Publishing a book not only gives you credibility in the marketplace but also makes your business more accessible by properly positioning your book on platforms like Amazon. Imagine that millions of people browse Amazon every day. With a book on this site, you reach the masses and inform them about your offer.

It's also a great way to give speeches, do interviews, and get recognized in an industry. From a credibility standpoint, publishing is also a way to share your knowledge and expertise on a particular topic. Similar to creating an online program or course, a book allows readers to access your knowledge, which can lead to increased sales and profitability for your business.

While many entrepreneurs know the importance of publishing a book, they don't know how to get started. Publishing a book is a marathon, not a sprint. It's important to have a professional team to help you write your book and with all other aspects, such as the various types of editing, cover and interior design, creating your own masthead, managing your publishing account, book marketing, and maximizing your investment.

That's exactly why we started Rogue Publishing Partners. We realized entrepreneurs need a place where they can find these services and be assured that the service providers are fully vetted and have years of experience in the publishing industry. At Rogue, we offer book coaching and publishing, ghostwriting, writing coaching, editing, book design, marketing, book launch, and author-related services like course creation and podcast development.

We often speak with previously published authors who have gone the "do-it-yourself" route or contracted with a service provider, which was a painful, frustrating process. At Rogue, we offer customized solutions so authors can choose the options that work best for them. Publishing isn't a one-size-fits-all proposition, and we see each book as an opportunity to spotlight the author and their business by bringing their expertise to the forefront.

Recently, we met with an author who self-published his book through an online platform and was having difficulty getting copies of his book. When we looked at his situation, we concluded it would be best to publish a second edition with new content, a new cover design, and a "teaser" for his second book. This way, the author can publish independently and maintain control of his book, publishing accounts, and marketing while promoting the second book. By looking at the big picture and understanding the entrepreneur's goals, we can create a plan that fits into his own marketing plan, budget, and schedule.

My company, Finish The Book Publishing, came about after I had worked in the publishing industry for several years and developed a business model that included a "white glove" educational element to guide entrepreneurs through the process of independent publishing and take the burden off their shoulders.

With over 30 years of experience in corporate America, I draw on experience in many industries, including human resources, marketing, television, and broadcasting. My experience benefits my clients by understanding their business goals and how a book can help them find their ideal clients.

Today, a few of us in the publishing industry created Rogue Publishing Partners (www.RoguePublishingPartners.com), where nonfiction authors can find talented, award-winning publishing professionals in one place. We offer both first-time and experienced authors customized solutions to their publishing needs, including business resources and connections through the Strategic Advisor Board (www.StrategicAdvisorBoard.com). The idea behind Rogue was to be a one-stop store for all your publishing needs, including ones you may not have thought of.

One of my favorite experiences was with a woman who provides feng shui decor for luxury homes and offices. She has an amazing story about her spiritual awakening, her family, and her business that keeps the reader turning the pages of her memoir. The great thing about this book is that we could incorporate her business branding and website and appeal to her ideal readership, which is also her target customer base. Now she's speaking to audiences about her journey and finding clients in the most unlikely places because they've read her book.

Another client is a successful personal injury attorney. She has written a book on preparedness and what to do legally and financially before an accident happens. The book is packed with great tips and strategies, but it ranked poorly on Amazon. We placed her book in better categories, ran a bestseller campaign for her, and she immediately had more book sales and customer leads because readers could find her book.

It gives me great joy to help authors publish a book they can be proud of that ties their story, brand, and community to a cause, mission, or movement. These are the good things that make the world a better place.

I love doing free consultations. Whether it's for my business or for Rogue, it's always exciting to meet someone new and learn about their book. Sometimes, entrepreneurs come to me with a finished manuscript and are ready for editing. Others have an idea for a book and a desire to write it themselves but need guidance on how to make their idea a reality. Finally, there are entrepreneurs who use our services for ghostwriting because they simply don't have enough time or don't feel like writing but know the benefits of being a published author.

A consultation is the first step in the right direction. We talk about the book, the business, and how it all fits together. If a more in-depth working session is needed, I offer a Book Visioning Session where I look at all the issues in the book to undo the outline and help the author get out of their head (linear thinking) and into their heart (emotions) to become a better writer and engage the reader.

The Rogue website (as well as the Finish the Book website) is the perfect way to show how we work with people who want to publish a book. The site is easy to navigate and offers packages for specific services like ghostwriting, editing, book design, and more. If there's something you're interested in, you can just click the "Consultation" button and make an appointment that suits you.

After the consultation, we can create a custom package for you that meets all your needs. This way, you can be flexible and not have to fit your book into a model that includes services you don't need.

Don't go it alone. Publishing a book is a rewarding experience if you have a good team that supports you, your mission, and your message. Books that are connected to a cause seem to do better in the marketplace, so think about what causes your business is connected to. By building a community around our businesses, we can create incremental change for the better, creating a ripple effect on humanity. Your book can do the same.

I've always said that we don't do our own dental work, right? The same is true for your book. Trust the professionals who guide you on your writing and publishing journey to give you the support you need to finish your book and be proud of your accomplishment. The results and the experience are worth it because your story matters.

About the Author

Known as The Transformational Book Coach for "cause publishing," Susie Schaefer believes that books are the gateway to creating a movement. Her love of books goes far beyond the feel of a fabric cover or the smell of a library. Whether writing a book helps an author heal past trauma or raise awareness for social change, Susie empowers storytellers to be part of the global conversation and create a ripple effect for humanity. Working with executives, coaches, consultants, entrepreneurs, and business owners brings her tremendous joy, particularly when an author shares their own personal story and how it connects to their mission, message, and community.

FLRRISH EMPOWERS PARENTS OF PREEMIE, NICU, AND SPECIAL NEEDS CHILDREN

JODI KLARINSTENFELD

My business is called FLRRiSH (pronounced flourish). It is a platform for preemie, NICU, and special needs parents. We seek to educate, empower, and support parents on their journey through the NICU and the years beyond by (1) helping educate them on the "different" growth and development timeline from full-term babies, (2) empowering them to advocate for themselves and their child, (3) coaching them on their journey, (4) providing resources for them, such as physical therapists, occupational therapists, speech therapists and other doctors and specialists of the like, and (5) perhaps most importantly, letting them know they are not alone.

Parents of preemie babies are often grouped together with those of full-term babies, even though their growth and development trajectories differ greatly. When a child is in the NICU or born early, more often than not, the parents also face many challenges. This is where FLRRiSH comes in - we help parents by providing knowledge and tools for navigating their complex journey. We offer emotional support for fatigued parents and knowledge that both empowers them and fosters informed engagement with hospital and school teams. With candor, patience, encouragement, and empathy, we are the helping hand preemie parents need.

FLRRiSH offers many solutions. We have three-to-five-minute stories told by other special needs preemie and NICU families that make parents feel less alone. We have state-by-state resource lists of therapists, doctors, and specialists for special needs NICU and preemie children. I also offer one-on-one coaching and coming soon, there will be group and public forums for additional support.

I believe what FLRRiSH offers is the best that's out there because it is the only resource and platform *by* a preemie and NICU parent *for* a preemie and NICU parent.

Because of this, every piece of advice is given solely from a parent's perspective and from a place of deep empathy and understanding. We hold parents' hands and let them know

that it's okay to feel upset, angry, and alone, but we also, in holding those hands, let them know that there is plenty of help out there for them and their children to become successful, grown adults.

FLRRiSH is a total passion project for me. As a preemie and NICU mom, I felt alone, overwhelmed, and frightened about what my motherhood journey was going to look like. I lacked then, and I still do now, that one person—that resource, that sounding board, that friend—to guide me and walk side by side with me throughout the process. Knowing there are many families out there in the world who have traveled a similar path, I knew I could not be the only one who felt this way.

Thus, I created FLRRiSH from what I felt was missing from my and my husband's NICU journey. Being a parent to any child is never easy, but being a parent to a child with extra needs and challenges is much more difficult. I continue to see the world as a glass half full. And I hope by helping others on their journeys that I can make their lives half full and make their journey easier than my own.

I find helping all preemie families so rewarding and cathartic. Whenever I talk to a mom and she says something like the following to me, I know that I have done my job. "Jodi, thank you for helping me enjoy being a mom. I can now appreciate motherhood and love my child because you have helped center me and feel not so alone and overwhelmed." Whenever I hear this, I smile and can't help but feel so wonderful inside, knowing I am helping others and making their journey less stressful than my own.

The best way for someone to *share* what I do is to write a testimonial, have me as a guest on their podcast, write articles about me, or have me on their TV show. I have been fortunate enough to have been a part of all the above, and I am going to be a guest speaker on my first panel soon. Invite me to an event of yours, share it on your social media, and help me spread the word about preemie parent awareness!

There are so many words of wisdom I can provide to parents out there. Foremost, I want to let them know they are not alone. With over 360,000 babies born prematurely every year, there are plenty of families going through something similar.

I also want parents to know that all children, whether or not they are born prematurely, have different growth trajectories and milestones. Just because someone is walking two months before your child is walking, it doesn't mean that the same child won't run faster than the early walker in the future.

It's also important to know that you and your child are much stronger than you ever can imagine. Just by showing up for your child every day, and checking your emotions at the door, you are giving your baby positive energy and positive feedback that can only serve them well as they travel down the road of life.

Equally, I think children who have a rough start and get extra love and support from their families can call on this energy when they face challenges later on. Life is difficult for everyone; it's how you manage and deal with it that matters. Being the parent of a preemie has made me appreciate everything in life much more, and it has given me a reset. I feel my daughter was born early so that I could turn my experience into something helpful for others.

The best way for someone to find me is online at www.flrrish.com. They can also follow me on Instagram, Facebook, TikTok, and LinkedIn as well at @FLRRiSH. Or they can email me at hello@flrrish.com.

About the Author

Jodi Klaristenfeld is a preemie parent advocate, thought leader, and niche consultant, and is disrupting the parent space with preemie education and empowerment.

HOW TO TAKE YOUR SOCIAL VIDEO AND PODCASTS TO THE NEXT LEVEL

KIM RITTBERG

I started my company after lying in my hospital delivery room and working on my phone. Instead of focusing on my son's birth, I was busy reading resumes and filling open jobs. I was leading a seventeen-person team, and it was growing great. It was very successful, but we went through a messy acquisition, and it was just chaos. I still had my job, and they had told me a big part of the acquisition was because of the video unit I built in this $100 million sale, but I realized I had lost what I wanted. I lost flexibility. I was successful, but this was not the picture of success that I wanted. I didn't want to be working while delivering my child. I wanted to work hard and have success and be ambitious, but on my own terms. I wanted to turn it off sometimes and get more control over my career. So, I decided to work for myself. It took two years to take that leap because doing something on your own is scary. But I'm doing it.

My background was as a journalist and a digital video executive producer, but now getting to teach small business owners how to grow their businesses has been really incredible. I've worked on some big video projects for companies and brands and getting to teach that to real estate agents, lawyers, doctors, and coaches has been so fun. I get to empower them and show them the opportunities that exist by coming up with new ideas. I'm teaching them how to think differently about content and then using that to grow their business.

My ideal customer is a small business owner or professional who's looking to grow their business strategically through social video and podcasts. Many of my clients have been doing video for a while but are looking to level up. I bring my experience as vice-president of branded content from PopSugar, a former journalist, and a Netflix executive to give their videos extra polish but also to think more strategically: What are new platforms to leverage? What are better ways to use the insights? How to look at podcasts in new ways to grow yourself as an expert and to grow your credibility and authority.

My ideal client's customer pain points come from the fact that social video can be so time-consuming and there comes a point where you feel almost out of ideas or your content is always the same, or maybe you feel you're selling too much. When I work with people, I try to get them out of their mindset, which is to default to sales or marketing content, and really lean into content-based marketing—coming up with

unique and creative ideas that will attract their ideal customer on social and then using that as an endpoint instead of more marketing-type of content or sales-based content. I specifically teach professionals and small business owners how to harness the power of video and podcasts to grow their businesses.

Social video can feel overwhelming, time-consuming, and even silly. A lot of professionals don't want to think about lip-syncing or dancing on video. And you don't have to do that. There are so many ways that you can grow your business with video. There's educational content, there's inspirational content, there's lifestyle style content. Once you understand how to think differently about content, there are all these great ideas out there that work for you and your niche and your industry.

Many people think it's going to take forever. It doesn't have to take that long, and it does not have to be expensive. You can film your footage on an iPhone with a ring light for really little money. To save even more time, film a bunch of content at the same time; this is called batch filming. If you can sit down and film four or eight videos in a row, you can sprinkle them across the next month or two of your content. That really helps get you a head start.

You should also batch your brainstorming process. When you're in the groove to be creative, take advantage of that. Come up with eight ideas and then write out the captions that you would match with them and try to edit several at the same time. Then, for the next few weeks, you don't even have to think about it. You can schedule your content and not have to worry about it. People think video is a huge weight, and that it's expensive and time-consuming. It really isn't. Once you understand how to do more with less, it's very empowering.

I work with my clients in both one-on-one and group coaching sessions. Some of my clients have been making videos for years and have hundreds of thousands of followers, and some have just gotten on social media and started showing their face on video. No matter where my clients are, I meet them where they're at. For people just starting out, it's a deep dive. It is everything you need to know to grow your business on social video and is offered in group or one-on-one coaching. I lay out how you can use social video to strategically grow your business, how to engage, how to make great content, how to come up with lots of content ideas, and how to make your videos look better—better lighting, better sound. It's a mindset shift. It's about understanding how content can change your business and then helping people get the creative juices flowing for brainstorms.

Another thing we do is focus on podcasts as an opportunity to grow your business and your brand. I'm working with some clients on podcasts because I think it's an incredible way to establish yourself as an expert, grow your network, and make really intimate and sincere connections throughout the industry. Not everyone understands how powerful podcasts can be. It can establish you as an authority. It can also automatically give you a lot of incredible social media content. You're having a podcast every week, and if you think creatively, you can come

up with a lot of additional content you can grow your business through.

Working with me is fantastic for a small business owner or a professional looking to grow their business. What I really love about this is that, having gone from journalism and marketing to now being a small business owner myself, I understand the pain of coming up with content for social media. I think we all feel that overwhelm, so I meet you where you are.

One of my clients said she signed with me because I make it fun. I really do. I'm very encouraging, and I have a strong background in camera media training. With video, it's about coming up with good ideas and also understanding how to appear on camera—how to be confident and credible.

Part of what I do is to help to build confidence by teaching on-camera skills in addition to the brainstorming and the production. It really is an all-in-one shop. For my customers who are more advanced, it's learning how to level up from what they've been doing that has been working, but maybe they still need to shake things up. Perhaps they're plateauing and need to come up with some new ideas again. I have another client who has 100,000 followers on Instagram, but she's looking to grow even more and bring in more paid clients. We think strategically, not just about views on social media but also if you are reaching your ideal client. Are you pushing them to buy? Are you pushing them to connect and thinking of new ways to do that? Every month, every year, there are new platforms and new ways

SOCIAL MEDIA

to reach your ideal client, build those relationships, bring those clients in, and close those deals.

I really feel the pain of small business owners because I am one, and I came from corporate, so I understand the fears, the pressures, and the stress. I am your coach and your executive producer in a box.

A recent win is with a client who is a real estate agent. He had enormous growth on TikTok with luxury-home videos, but he also had years of experience in the industry. I wanted to focus on the education angle but make it fun. We shot this incredible series of videos with different educational aspects to it of New York City, and he got a client a multimillion-dollar referral deal, specifically from the social videos that he saw. And overall, across his social media, he's grown a huge referral business. It's been a huge win for his bottom line to level up, and invest his time, energy, and his money into social video.

I have another client whose reels on Instagram were getting about 100 views. I taught her how to think about content and how to be more creative and peg a news hook into the content. She made a reel about Rihanna and the Super Bowl because I told her it was a good opportunity to get new eyeballs to her brand. She ended up getting 13,000 views on that reel because she thought differently about content.

I think it's really about readjusting the mindset to think more like a journalist and less like a marketer. That's one of the biggest things. But my biggest tip is to get on camera. I have been told by clients I'm really fun to work with and very encouraging. Realize you can do it. It is worth it. There's very little risk, and the risk is worth the reward. What you put in, you get out; I've seen it time and again with my clients.

My clients are getting speaking gigs. They're getting more clients. They're growing their revenue through video and podcasts. It's out there for the taking. I host a podcast called *Mom's Exit Interview*. I was hesitant because I knew a weekly podcast would be a lot of work, but I believed in the idea, and I followed through on it. From the podcast, I have tripled my paid speaking engagements and have landed many clients. I've landed clients through social video. I'm a walking advertisement for the power of social video and podcasts, and so are my clients.

Get on video! Everyone hates the sound of their voice. Everyone hates how they look on camera. Everyone feels out of ideas, and everyone feels overwhelmed. But you have to realize it's a great tool for your business. It's never been easier. All you need is an iPhone and an understanding of how to create great content. So get on video and learn how to tell stories that are interesting and not just sales and marketing. Think of content differently. *What would I read in a magazine? What videos would I actually click on? Would I click on "Work with me because..." or would I click on "Four reasons why..."*

Do not fear social media, do not fear video, and do not fear podcasts. They are powerful tools to grow your network, client base, and fan base. You have to be out there, you have to put yourself on video, and you have to think outside the box to really cut through the noise. Once you learn you can do it, you can absolutely grow your business.

If someone wants to work with me, they should go to my website at kimrittberg.com. Drop me a line on my contact form or schedule a meeting with me. My website has a huge portfolio of work I've done and also testimonials of people who've worked with me and how the experience was.

About the Author

Kim Rittberg helps independent professionals and brands be better on-camera and make unforgettable video and podcast content to grow their business. She is an award-winning video and content expert working across social media, TV, digital video, and podcasts. She spent fifteen years as a media executive at Netflix, *PEOPLE Magazine*, and in TV news and launched the first-ever video unit for *Us Weekly*. Kim has been featured in *Business Insider* and *Fast Company* and has been a speaker and instructor at UPENN and Syracuse University and is a graduate of the University of Pennsylvania Annenberg School. She also hosts *Mom's Exit Interview* podcast, spurred by her decision to quit corporate and launch her own business after working in the hospital while giving birth to her second child. The podcast helps women craft careers that work for their life—instead of the other way around.

STARTING A DIGITAL MARKETING AGENCY AMIDST A PANDEMIC

TATIANA CHAMORRO

I was born in Nicaragua, but my husband and I moved to the United States in 2014. Our reason for moving was for my husband to pursue a master's degree in business administration. He completed the program within a year, which gave me the opportunity to enroll in a university as well. After four years, I was able to finish both my undergraduate and master's degrees without any student debt. It was after this achievement that I began my journey as an entrepreneur.

In the midst of the pandemic in 2020, I launched my marketing agency, which has since flourished. That same year, we merged with Hite, creating the first digital marketing franchise in the United States. I became the main founder of Hite Creative, a division within Hite International, which now boasts twenty-five locations and a workforce of two hundred. As of now, I hold a position on the board of Hite International and am the CEO of Hite Digital Dallas, the franchise I currently own.

In the past few years, we have experienced significant growth and have been learning what it takes to be successful business owners and entrepreneurs. Along with this, we also ventured into real estate investing, expanding our portfolio from eleven single-family homes to three apartment complexes since 2017. I am also exploring what a philanthropic journey looks like for me, and my husband and I have recently launched our first scholarship at the university we attended when we first arrived in Dallas, Texas in 2014. This is why I am where I am today, and it's a little bit about what motivates me to continue on this path.

One of my favorite success stories is about someone who started working with me. In 2020, I co-founded Hite Creative as a separate company, which later merged into Hite International. The very first person we hired for Hite Creative was a friend I knew from college in Nicaragua. Although I finished my undergraduate studies in the United States, I had always wanted to create a team in Nicaragua that could provide services to clients in the United States.

When the franchise model was introduced, I saw an opportunity to pitch the idea of a creative division to my business partner. This division would offer services such as logo design, branding manuals, and website creation to any of our franchisees. This idea became a reality, and it has enabled us to create a space where talented and creative individuals can thrive.

Approximately three months after launching, we hired our first branding manager, who happened to be the woman I mentioned earlier. In the beginning, we worked together long hours, and I mentored her on how to achieve the level of quality that we needed to satisfy our clients in the United States. However, after only three months, she was leading conversations and projects, and now she manages our entire branding division with a team of five employees.

It has been thrilling to watch her become an exceptional professional and leader. She is currently mentoring some of our design employees who started in a similar position to where she began, and this has been the most rewarding aspect of my role as an entrepreneur. It made me realize that my passion lies in helping people grow and find happiness in what they do.

My target audience consists of experienced business owners who have been in the industry for more than three years, earning an annual revenue of around $300,000 or more. They are interested in increasing their business's valuation, raising brand awareness, or acquiring new clients through digital marketing strategies. However, they often struggle with uncertainty about how to utilize digital marketing tools effectively and obtain a positive return on investment from their online strategies.

We offer a range of services to our clients, including branding, web design and development, SEO, Google ads, and Facebook ads. However, before we commence any service, we conduct a thorough audit of their online presence. This audit covers their website, any previous ad campaigns, and social media platforms. After evaluating these factors and asking them specific questions, we create a personalized marketing strategy that aligns with their goals and their specified investment. Our aim is to help them achieve their objectives and remain within their financial boundaries.

While we are not the only marketing agency in the industry, we distinguish ourselves by focusing on ROI. This means that we collect

data on the outcomes of our marketing strategies, including SEO results, website traffic sources, conversion rates, and the number of paying clients. We analyze how these factors impact the bottom line of our client's business, which is their revenue.

Based on this analysis, we make adjustments to our marketing strategies as necessary. For instance, after running SEO and Facebook ads for six months, we found that SEO generated the most significant ROI. Although Facebook ads were not losing money, they were not as profitable as SEO. We discussed this with our client and developed a strategy that made sense for the next few months, ensuring that they received a positive return on their investment and made the most of our services.

When I first ventured into entrepreneurship, I had no idea what it would entail. It was an intimidating and isolating experience, but it was also fascinating and stimulating. What I enjoyed the most was the opportunity to collaborate with individuals, help businesses grow and witness them succeed. If I didn't have a passion for my work, it would have been easy to give up.

For those considering entrepreneurship, it is essential to enter a field that resonates with your passions. I am not only referring to doing what you like but to something greater. What motivates you? What drives your purpose? Having clarity on these questions will provide confidence when you dive into the world of entrepreneurship.

Additionally, it is crucial to surround yourself with a support system. Building a team that can guide you through the entrepreneurial journey is imperative, as the process can be lonely at times. Working with like-minded individuals can provide a sense of community and help overcome obstacles with more skill and determination. Therefore, I encourage anyone embarking on this journey to find a group of individuals who share your vision and can offer support during difficult times.

I'm a marketer, so you can probably find me almost anywhere. I'm on Instagram, and LinkedIn, but you can also go to my website, www.tiana.chamorro.com, and you can schedule a time to meet with me. I recommend you schedule a marketing strategy plan. We do that just by you answering a couple of questions and then we'll present it to you. And that's where the relationship can really begin. You can also look at our website, hitedigital.com/dallas.

About the Author

Tatiana Chamorro is a mother, investor, and multi-faceted entrepreneur. She is the CEO of Hite Digital Dallas, an industry-leading agency in brand design and marketing services. Tatiana is also the founder of Hite Creative, a division of Hite International, a team of over two hundred team members, serving twenty-five locations across the United States. Tatiana is passionate about helping people, businesses, and brands overcome growth barriers with strategic solutions so they can reach their desired success.

EMPOWERING WOMEN TO TAKE CONTROL OF THEIR LIVES

CORINNE MORAHAN

Despite the common goal of creating order through organization, most people have tried many approaches without success. However, in The Grid + Glam Home Organizing Membership, our approach is based on practical research that goes beyond the benefits of organizing and centers on how to achieve a lasting transformation. By including gamification, support, and accountability, we ensure everyone can succeed.

The foundation of this program is working with your mindset. We invest a lot of time in developing the right mindset before we even dive into the work, so you understand the practical steps of decluttering and organizing. Understanding the reasoning behind the steps we take has proven to be a major indicator of success.

We also encourage family and friends to get involved to ensure that the work is done together rather than in isolation. This ensures the results achieved are maintained long-term. We are the first solution of this kind in the market, and while there are similar programs, none offer the same level of support and accountability. The only better option for those that aren't in DIY programs might be to hire a professional organizer to come into your home to do the organizing for you. Grid + Glam has a team of organizers who travel the country and love creating that transformation for our clients. For those who would like to do it themselves or can't afford to hire a professional organizer, joining The Grid + Glam Home Organizing is the best solution.

The Grid + Glam Home Organizing Membership is a revolutionary digital program designed to help women organize their homes and their lives over twelve months. As an online membership, members log in each week to access the new resources provided. We drip out the content so as not to overwhelm our members, and we concentrate on a single room, or sometimes two, at a time and leverage our four-step process to achieve our goals.

The first step involves addressing our mindset because transformation cannot occur if our thinking is not aligned. The second step requires decluttering by getting rid of items that no longer serve a purpose or that we no longer cherish or use. Then, we develop an organizing system that is customized to your life. Finally, we use the "reset" phase to maintain all your hard work. Our proprietary approach has hundreds of testimonials and truly works because it is broken down into bite-sized segments.

Our community is supportive, and we work together as we tackle each space. We celebrate each other's successes and cheer each other on. Our team is available to offer customized coaching and check-ins, and our membership forum allows members to share obstacles and get advice from other members. The program consists of short videos that can be watched at your convenience, and we provide checklists to help you stay on track. Most importantly, we provide the support and accountability that comes from being part of an incredible community.

I can relate to our ideal client avatar so well because I was once her. I had a successful career on Wall Street, a loving husband, two beautiful children, and was living in our dream home in the Boston suburbs. Yet, despite all this, I was unhappy. The endless list of responsibilities that came with my life left me feeling drained, and it took away any joy or pleasure that I should have been experiencing.

After spending a year decluttering and organizing my home, my life was transformed. I implemented systems that allowed me to free up my time and that created a ripple effect. Not only did I declutter toxic relationships and thought patterns, but I also became a happier and better person, wife, and mother. The transformation I experienced inspired me to leave my career on Wall Street and start a business that could help others achieve similar results.

As I approached my 40th birthday, I knew it was now or never to take that leap of faith.

I'm thrilled that I did. Grid + Glam has now grown into a seven-figure business, and we have helped nearly 1,000 people go through our membership program. We impact thousands of lives daily through our social channels. Our success is a testament to the power of organization and the value of creating a life that truly brings us joy.

Our goal is to transform the world, one person at a time. We focus on empowering women to recognize that their to-do list does not dictate their and that their happiness is within their control. We believe individuals have the power to say no to unnecessary responsibilities and consumption in their lives. We encourage peeling back layers and creating space in our lives. This does not mean adopting a minimalist lifestyle, as we believe in enjoying the luxury items we purchase. Our mission is to enable individuals to savor life's moments and fully appreciate the luxuries they have without feeling weighed down by unnecessary clutter or responsibility.

At Grid + Glam, our ideal client is a high-performing woman who has lost her passion for life because of an overwhelming to-do list and responsibilities. She recognizes that, with the right system, she can regain her joy and bring passion back into her life. If she has children, she understands that getting organized will help her return to her pre-mom self. She may have attempted to get organized in the past but has struggled to maintain any system, and now she is eager to learn a new approach.

Our ideal client is excited to receive coaching throughout the process and be part of a supportive community of women undergoing the same journey. She thrives when working on bite-sized tasks, being held accountable, and having a clear checklist to guide her. Ultimately, she is ready to organize her home, allowing her to appreciate the abundance in her life to the fullest.

Our home-organizing membership helps transform our members' lives by providing a structured and methodical approach to decluttering and organizing their home, one room at a time, over the course of a year. We understand that life can be unpredictable, which is why our program is flexible and accessible for even the busiest individuals. With built-in support, gamification, and celebration, our program offers our customers the tools and resources they need to finally achieve their organizing goals and take control of their life. With nearly 1,000 successful participants, we know that our approach works and can truly make a difference in transforming one's mindset and home.

We love to share the story of one of our early members who had struggled with organizing her home and felt like a failure despite trying many times in the past. As a wife and mother of a child with ADHD, and a recent diagnosis of being on the autism spectrum herself, organization was challenging and was affecting her mental health. However, after joining the Grid + Glam Home Organization Membership, she could completely declutter and organize her home, which gave her a newfound confidence in her abilities as a mother and wife. The transformation was so profound that she went from considering herself a "hot mess" to becoming a professional organizer. The membership not only transformed her personal life and relationships but also became the foundation for her successful business.

All of our programs are on our website at www.gridandglam.com. Have a look around and see what programs we offer that might be a great fit. If you have any questions, you can ask them through the contact form. I'm always hanging out on Instagram in my DMs: @gridandglam. Shoot me a DM and tell me you read this story and that you would love to find out how we could work together!

Our program has gained a lot of attention and positive feedback, largely because of social media, particularly Instagram and Tik-Tok. We are thrilled when people share our content on their social channels, as it helps to spread the word about our mission. For those with an active email list, like our own list of over 20,000 people, we welcome the opportunity to be featured in newsletters and introduced to new audiences. We recognize there are always women out there who could benefit from our services, and we are grateful for any opportunity to connect with them.

I hope that you realize you are amazing, and this truth is the foundation for anything you want to accomplish. No matter how many times you've tried and fallen short, there is always a chance to try again, to learn from the past, and to find a new way. You can transform your life and achieve your goals, no matter your current situation. It may not be easy, and it will take time and effort, but it's all about consistency. By taking small, manageable steps each day, you'll be amazed at how much progress you make. You deserve to live the life you want, and you have what it takes to get there. Believe in yourself and start taking action today.

About the Author

Corinne Morahan is a professional organizer and business coach, leading the industry in strategies to take action and create a life you love. As the founder and CEO of Grid + Glam®, her work has been featured in The Boston Globe, Architectural Digest, New York Magazine, HGTV Magazine, NBC News, and more. Corinne earned a bachelor's degree from the University of Michigan and a master's degree from Harvard University. She began her career working on Wall Street and currently lives just outside Boston, MA, with her husband and two children.

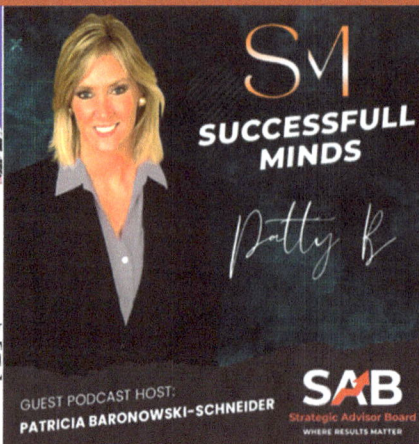

A NEW LOVE POWERED MISSION

STACI MILLARD

I started my first business in 2013 because I had a burning desire to increase the standards. I wanted to do better for clients. I wanted to do better for my future employees. And I wanted to do better for my family.

I started with a laptop in my basement, going to my clients to help them, and very quickly, business exploded. Within eight years, I and my laptop in the basement became a ten-person team, a full-fledged office that was making over seven figures in revenue every year. And the best part, even better than just doing well for my clients and team, I was also doing great things for the community.

During my time running my accounting firm, I fell in love with helping small businesses succeed. Aside from taxes and accounting, I could see what kind of extra help was needed. That led me to organize events for women where we helped women entrepreneurs with everything they needed to be successful. Sometimes it was mindset, and sometimes it was strategy in a different area, but we took care of them, and I loved doing that.

As time went on, I found I was so committed to small businesses and their success that I lost the desire to do the tax work. By the end of 2020, I was burnt out, even though on paper I had it all. Most people think burnout only happens when you work too many hours, but that wasn't the case for me. It was because I was doing something that I didn't have a desire to do. I was working normal hour days, taking vacations, and making money, but something was missing. So, I started thinking about what I could do to make my business more fun.

I looked at my business as it was and realized that I would have to tear most of it apart to rebuild something I wanted. I felt like I was doing it an injustice because it was a great business, and another accountant would be thrilled to own the firm I had built. I put it up for sale, and it sold quickly. To have built and sold a seven-figure business was validation that the strategies and mindsets I had been preaching to my clients and using on myself in fact worked to create not only a great business for me but one that could create wealth for my family and be passed on.

After selling my firm, I dove into creating a space that focused on small business owners through mentorship, community, and education. Being able to spend more time developing leaders and helping them implement their plans was everything I had been missing. We don't just set a plan and suddenly it works; we often must adjust it as we go along. I now have the time and the opportunity to do that.

After working with thousands of businesses, I can tell you one theme that stands out is that most of us are not experienced in business. We are great at our trade but running a business based on that skill is a whole new ball game. While we're trying to do everything, we're also learning along the way. When you start out, you don't have a team of experts taking care of everything. You're the one making decisions, often about things for which you don't have the skills to really make the best decisions.

In addition to having to develop skills you didn't realize you would have to learn, a lot of advice falls on deaf ears because it comes at the wrong time. What I mean is there are different levels of business. If you're at the beginning of your business, you need something very different than if you've been at it for five or six years. If you get the advice at the wrong time, it can have a negative impact.

For example, if you're five or six years into the business and you have a team, you need to set up the infrastructure and the systems, so the business isn't dependent on you anymore. You can't keep track of everything that's going on, so those systems are necessary. If you had received that advice at year one or two, the time you spent on systems would have hindered sales and held you back instead of propelling you forward. In comparison, at year five or six, if you have received advice to focus on sales, which is what that one-to-two-year business needed, that's a problem, because when you make more sales, you take all your systems problems with you. When you're small, those systems problems don't stand out as much because you have your hands much closer to everything. So, you can see that taking the wrong advice based on your stage of business can really hurt how quickly you reach your goals, if at all.

Another great example is comparing a start up with stage two business that's two to three years in. At the startup stage, we often see businesses charging slightly under their competition and offering a bit more. They can do this because they typically are running lean and have great profit margins, so despite charging less, they are making a bit more. The lower prices they charge act as a catalyst to grow their business which they obtain testimonials and referrals for, and it helps them grow.

But a couple years into scaling, they become more complex and need to raise prices to make the same profits. If the startup was told to raise prices, they wouldn't have scaled as quickly. And if the stage 2 business was told to keep with the "do more, charge less" model, they would work terribly hard for low profits. Again, well-intended advice at the wrong stage of business can do more harm than good.

This is where my work comes in. I teach you how to run a small business well, and I bring in other experts from different industries where I don't have expert level experience. Together, we help you understand what it takes to be a successful CEO. We believe it's important to have an income and make an impact without burning out. You need to acquire new skills. You need to learn marketing. You need to learn how to sell. You

need to learn business strategy. You need to understand finance. You need to understand HR. You need to know how to be a leader. You probably weren't taught how to motivate people, how to lead well, and how to have difficult conversations when needed. Bringing all of that together to create a strong leader for a company that is tied to its mission and makes money is complicated, but it can be done. Many companies have done it before you, and I know you can learn it, also.

Some of the greatest success stories in my work are the ones that have ripple effects. Working with the social media agency that was able to feel good about themselves as leaders, create smooth systems that satisfied both the owner, employees, and clients. The changes allowed them to pay above-industry average wages to their employees. That's impact. The businesses that they serve then get great quality service and increase their own impact in the world.

Another business I work with provides physical and mental health support. The work we do together allows them to give back to their community and frees up administrative time to have more impact on patients. The work we do together creates a happy business, and everyone wins.

I'm passionate about showing business owners that they really can have it all. It doesn't have to be a struggle. I ran a business that had it all, so it's important to show people it can be done and then invest in them and put those building blocks in place.

I think one of the hardest struggles is that everyone wants to become successful overnight, but like any other skill or profession, it rarely works that way. Hairdressers don't get good at hairdressing overnight. Massage therapists must train for a certain number of hours. We develop these skills over time, and so it is with running a business. It's hard to fight the "have a successful business overnight" message, but if someone will put in the effort and develop their skills, that's where the magic happens.

There are a few things that set my work apart, but the two most important are that I always look at finances and I don't just provide ideas, I help create and implement plans. A lot of other advice out there can be short-sighted. I have clients come to me after working with a sales coach or a marketing coach, and they have been told they have a great product people will love, so they focus all their efforts with that coach on selling. But without the full business strategy being looked at, there are holes in the plan. You end up working countless hours, feeling unfulfilled, making little to no profit, and you end up feeling like giving up. There is an entire system that goes into supporting the delivery of each sale and the businesses should be treated as a whole instead of being seen only in fractional pieces. My system is holistic. I bring the finances together and look at how you can make money and make a difference at the same time, how you can put your heart into your community, and how you can live a good life in the process.

At the highest level, I help businesses scale through one-on-one mentoring. I bring together the three pillars of making money, having an impact, and living a great life, and then I start crafting your specific business model so you can have it all. More importantly, I support you in making the changes that are required to get there. I have a couple of in-between tiers that support entrepreneurs through strategy sessions and masterminds, creating help no matter what stage you're at.

One of the best ways to be introduced to my work is through Small Business School workshops or podcast. I offer workshops monthly that are free to attend live. The school's workshops revolve around all facets of small business, and every month there's a different topic. You can attend live for free, or we offer a monthly membership for $99 if you want to watch the replays and attend the twice-monthly office hours sessions. I love the incredible value that is provided and hearing the difference being made no matter the level you invest at.

To end this all with a twist, I've added more of my own businesses to the mix. I love my work in mentorship but there is a part of me that felt if I was only mentoring businesses, I might lose touch with what it was like to be in the trenches as a small business owner. In June 2022, I saw a company for sale that fit my family. It was called Love Powered Co., and it offered decks of affirmation cards for women and children. Their goal was to change the way our future leaders work—how mindful they were and how emotionally resilient they were. I loved the mission. I used the product in my family and saw the impact the company could have on the world, so I took a leap and purchased the business. I am an entrepreneur at heart, and I love the passion I have to shape the mission of this company, steer its impact on the world, and use the skills I've developed helping thousands of other businesses over the years.

I hope you will follow along with the journey, watching Love Powered Co. scale its impact. I hope you will learn from the School for Small Business podcast or attend a live training from Small Business School. Most importantly, I hope these words have taught you that entrepreneurship is a beautiful journey of aligning your business with your heart, and when you do that, you can truly have it all.

About the Author

Staci Millard is a seven-figure business owner and multi-passionate entrepreneur. She is obsessed with seeing small businesses succeed with having massive income and impact while living a life they are lit up about.

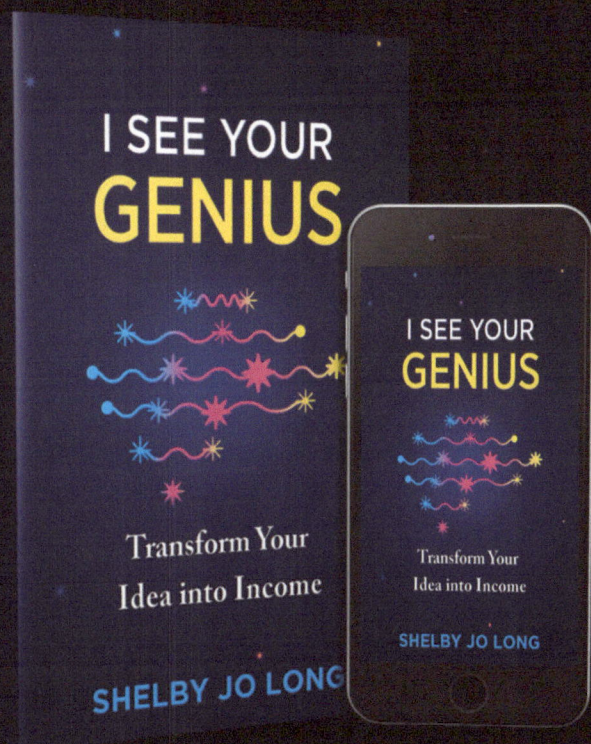

FROM PEACE CORPS VOLUNTEER TO CEO: THE COVEDOZA STORY

ELISA MOLINA

COVEDOZA is a company close to my heart, and I want to share with you how it came about. The idea came from my time in the Peace Corps in Costa Rica. I worked in a rural community called Guaitil de Santa Cruz, where I became an Economic Community Development Advisor. I helped local artisans who made a living from their craft, but I soon found that competition among them was doing more harm than good. Some community members felt people were stealing each other's customers and tourists, which wasn't true. After three years, I realized that the solution was to create cooperatives and raise community awareness.

I used English teaching as a way to tell the stories of artisans, and COVEDOZA was born. I wanted to support artisans of all kinds, not just those who worked with pottery, because I believed art has the power to heal. Art is a way for people to express themselves and feel seen and validated.

I returned home after my service and a few years later, I had the idea to create a platform to collaborate with artists. On our blog and social media, we share stories and photos that help clients connect with artists on a deeper level.

Our collaboration with artists also provides them with economic opportunities. We pay artists an agreed-upon percentage of each product sold from their collection. We focus on marketing their products, their art, and their stories, while the artists can focus on their craft and business growth. We also pay the artists quarterly passive income for the year we work with them. We've been doing this for four years now, since March 2019, and I'm proud of what we've accomplished. I'm excited to see how much more COVEDOZA can accomplish with the support of our customers.

Our mission at COVEDOZA is to empower women and nonbinary individuals who identify as feminists to express themselves through art and fashion. We target the 18 million women between the ages of 25 and 45 who believe in feminist ideals and want to make a difference in their community.

Customers recognize that fast fashion isn't sustainable and want to do something for the environment by being more conscious about the products they buy. Our print-on-demand model fights fast fashion and combines the sustainability of slow fashion with artistic skills to solve this problem.

We know that women often feel that their voices are being silenced, and that's where COVEDOZA comes in. We give them the tools and resources to express themselves through clothing and accessories that spark conversations in everyday life. We believe that art is a path to healing, and our platform allows artists to showcase their art while creating economic opportunities for them.

We've been doing this for four years now and have made great strides. Our approach has created a deeper connection with our customers so that the purchase is no longer just a transaction, but a transformation. Our work with artists has opened up economic opportunities for them while we focus on marketing their products, their art, and their stories. We're proud of what we have accomplished so far and look forward to continuing to make a difference with the support of our customers.

COVEDOZA is a brand that connects customers with women artists through their purchases on covedoza.com. We want our customers to know the story behind the products they buy. We share information about the artists' work and their stories so that our customers can learn more about the women who support them.

At COVEDOZA, we strive to create a platform that brings together feminist consumers who care about social justice, representation, and gender inequality in the arts. We focus on highlighting women artists of color through our print collaborations and empowering our customers to express themselves and be inspired by our products. Our product line includes apparel, accessories, drinkware, stationery, and digital art.

When you support COVEDOZA, you not only receive quality products, but you also actively take part in a movement that empowers women and promotes social justice. We believe we can change the world by supporting women artists and giving them a platform to have their voices heard.

At COVEDOZA, we believe in the power of coming together as a community. We don't believe in gatekeeping. Instead, we want to share the knowledge we've learned to help others on their path to success. Over the past few years, we've raised more than $43,000 through grants and crowdfunding to partner with organizations like the Latin American Association and the Georgia Hispanic Chamber of Commerce. Together, we host free workshops for low-income women in Georgia to learn about how to start their own businesses or apply for grants to grow their existing businesses.

I've been fortunate to lead workshops both online and in person for these hardworking women who want to create economic opportunities for themselves and their families. I teach them tips and tricks to help them get funding similar to what I've received here in Georgia. These workshops have made a big difference, and I'm thrilled when I hear success stories from participants, such as one woman who received the Comcast Rise Award and another who received a $5,000 grant after I guided her through the application process for the Elevate Together grant.

These stories remind me why we need to share information and help others fulfill their dreams through our experiences. We want to help others heal and grow in their entrepreneurial journey. It has been a blessing to support these amazing women, and we look forward to continuing to do so in the future.

If you want to learn more about COVEDOZA, the best way to find us is online. You can follow us on social media at @covedosa and visit our website at covedosa.com. You can read our story on the About Us page on our website. If you connect with our story, you can support the artists we work with by making a purchase. Your purchase will help them grow and invest in their craft.

If you're interested in working with me, I offer virtual cafecitos, which are virtual coffee breaks. In these paid one-on-one sessions, I guide you on your journey and answer any questions you have. For example, I can help you find funding, start a business, or create a lifestyle product on Shopify.

To get the word out about COVEDOZA, here are a few things you can do. First, take the time to learn more about our work and mission. If you're drawn to our stories, share our work on social media by spreading the word about our content. When you purchase a product, you learn about the artists who create these works and the impact your purchase has on them.

If you want to help us grow, we also welcome any connections you can make, whether it's with a magazine or a mentor or just by letting us know about opportunities we can take advantage of. Your time is valuable, and we want to make sure it's well spent. When you take the time to share our work, network with others, or give us feedback on how we can improve, it really makes a difference.

Starting a business can be difficult, but I've learned that the only way to know if it'll be successful is to take action. Be willing to apply for grants and put your ideas into action, even if they aren't perfect. Being an entrepreneur requires flexibility, ingenuity, and most importantly, passion. There will be obstacles and naysayers, but if you believe in yourself and your vision, you can overcome them.

Remember that starting a business is a journey, not a destination. It's important you stay focused and motivated, even when things get tough. You may experience setbacks and disappointments along the way, but don't let them discourage you. Keep going and take care of business.

Remember that perfectionism can hold you back. You don't have to have it all figured out before you start. It's better to be proactive and learn as you go. Be willing to make mistakes and learn from them.

Ultimately, only through trial and error can you find out if entrepreneurship is really for you. Don't let fear or laziness hold you back. Take the first step and see where it takes you. Remember that the only way is through.

About the Author

Elisa Molina is the founder and CEO of COVEDOZA, an e-commerce platform that connects customers with women artists worldwide. Her experiences in the Peace Corps inspired her to create a platform that uses digital art to highlight feminism, social justice, and gender inequalities in art. Her work has been recognized with several awards, including the 2020 Latino Small Business Resilience Award and the 2023 Entreprenista 100 Award. Elisa was also selected for the American Express and IFundWomen 100 for 100 'Founders of Change' Grant Program and was the 2021 winner of the Jefes del Futuro Contest hosted by Cricket Wireless. In addition, she was nominated for the Entrepreneur of the Year Award by the Latin America Association.

UNLOCKING YOUR FULL POTENTIAL WITH ADORATHERAPY

LAURA MCCANN

Our ideal client is someone who is working on their personal transformation. They're interested in healing themselves and are looking for new methods such as aura and chakra balancing, aromatherapy, energy work such as Reiki and yoga, or meditation. An open mind, attraction to mindful practices, and a desire for growth to become the best self are common characteristics of our guests. We work with people of all ages and their pets.

Whether it's anxiety, stress, grief, trauma, or just everyday life, most of us have something we can work on to become more balanced and powerful without burning out. We know when you remember your thoughts create your reality, you'll begin a new journey of self-acceptance. You'll finally know that you're DIVINE. You'll finally admire yourself! We're here to remind our guests that they can become their own healers.

Transformation is at the heart of ADORAtherapy's mission. It's based on the belief that Mother Earth's abundant resources can transform the human experience. We combine auratherapy with aromatherapy:

Our aroma perfumes lift and change your mood in the moment, allowing you to find your best self. When we have the presence of mind and heart to be more loving and compassionate toward ourselves, this feeling cascades into the world and everything we touch in it. When we individually transform ourselves into the best version of ourselves, we weave a new tapestry for humanity that ultimately raises our collective consciousness. The Alkemie, Moodzee, Chakra Boost, and Room Boost collections bring you back to your healthy center and purpose. Our aroma perfumes awaken your senses. As an alternative to traditional perfume, these natural fragrances and body care products with their uniquely formulated essential oils and absolutes are the perfect tool to support your practice of breath and affirmation. The expertly formulated fragrances help you manage stress, anxiety, motivation, focus, spirituality, and more. Think of aroma-perfume as your life coach in a bottle.

Utilizing the newest techniques, our stunning 3D Aura imaging software displays aura and chakra results simultaneously. Our powerful software displays data from a scanner and provides a series of beautifully detailed charts and graphs that allow our guests to gain insight into their body, mind and spirit.

SMELL + BRAIN

There is a powerful connection between the sense of smell and the limbic center of our brain, which regulates our physiology, including mood, memory, and emotions. When breathing in essential oil blends of pure plant aromas, we can literally transform how we feel in the moment, positively shifting the way we relate to ourselves, our personal and professional relationships, and ultimately, the world around us.

ELEVATES MOOD + FEELINGS

We pay great attention to green tenets of business and focus on sustainability by choosing organic, biodynamic, and wildcrafted growing methods. With proper planting, growing, harvesting, and distilling techniques, the quintessence of each plant is nurtured and brought forth for proper use. These plants grow to embody their perfection and fulfill their ability to transform, rejuvenate and balance the human condition.

BE YOUR BEST SELF

By creating formulas with aromatics from plant products around the world, we aim to stimulate the senses in a way that awakens the joys and passions of humanity. The better we feel, the more this creates a bridge that allows our greatest self-expression to surface. We believe in the motto: "We must be the change we want to see in the world."

Transform your mood. Transform your awareness. Transform your consciousness.

Coherence. Root. Subtle bodies. Auratherapy.

Those are some of the words Asheville shopkeeper and Chief Mood Booster Laura McCann effortlessly bandies about during an aura session at ADORAtherapy at the Grove Arcade downtown. It's to be expected, really. That "chief" title is no joke, and she's earned it after more than twenty years as a C-suite executive in the fashion and technology industries.

Becoming a "Life Coach in a Bottle" has been a lifetime in the making:

- Laura's journey from child actress in Miami, where she was born
- To her teens living in Paris as a "French movie star"
- To New York, where she graduated from Parsons School of Design and started her first business at 28 years old

Figuring out who she was and how to live her best life wasn't a "nice to have," it was a "have to have." Especially considering she often had to know herself well enough not to self-destruct.

Laura, 59, founded ADORAtherapy to sell aroma-perfume directly to her customers. In the early years of the company, Laura's role focused more on the business side and back office, handling marketing, manufacturing, sourcing, and finance. After many years of healing herself with alternative and integrative medicine, she realized her calling isn't just business, her true calling is to remind people to adore themselves.

"Loving ourselves is a way to break away from the beliefs and patterns that make us small and unhappy. ADORAtherapy is not traditional therapy, it's breathwork combined with intention and the desire to heal ourselves. You are the therapist and you control the outcome: your vibrational energy and your mood."

When ADORAtherapy opened its first store in Asheville in November 2021, Laura came from behind the scenes to the front lines. ADORAtherapy offers a unique experience, aura readings and chakra balancing. Using 3D software, her partner Jim Levinson, the company's Chief Auratherapist, scans clients and reveals their true colors. After an in-depth session to discuss the results of the aura and chakra analysis, Laura introduces the healing powers of aromatherapy with a breathwork session.

"The Auratherapy Studio came to be because my life partner Jim wanted to retire and do more healing work. He studied Reiki and Chi energy and even became an ordained minister. And the more we thought about how his third act would look, the vision of combining what we both wanted became so clear."

"Having a conversation without finding out what is truly meaningful seems like a missed opportunity," says Laura, something she does often, as she explains how she ended up a shopkeeper instead of continuing to scale businesses while sitting behind a desk.

Calm and cool, yet social and communicative, Laura is always engaging—and engaged. She's approachable in a chic, hippie way. It's something that probably comes naturally, given her Parisian flair and American gift of gab. "I'm always interested in what makes people tick," she admits.

She also doesn't use her obvious intellect like a hammer. Laura uses her intelligence to help people get better. "At the store, we work with people to raise their awareness and consciousness. We remind them that they're energetic beings."

- A family comes into the shop and the mother asks if we know a way to help her teenage son be in a better mood. After an aura reading and a healing session, the son opens up. He's autistic and is totally excited about the reading, the laptop, and his crystal. His mother is thrilled. He has opened his throat chakra and his heart.
- She chats with a woman who comes for a hostess gift and ends up in a deep conversation and a hug.
- A mother and daughter reunited after Covid treat themselves to an aura photo session, and Laura shows them aspects of their report, which includes a graph representing their seven chakras, reveals to them aspects of their personalities and areas of improvement that are so spot on. To the point where everyone gets goosebumps, especially Laura, who is intuitive. The goosebumps are confirmation that "what is being said and shared is true," she says.

We're so fortunate. Every day we work with energy, and we can transform someone's day, even their life.

"Aromatherapy is coming back into vogue and being reactivated because we're overwhelmed by too many synthetic fragrances," she says.

"We've lost our noses, in some cases our sense of smell, after Covid. Essential oils can be blended into beautiful scents that heal. Functional ingredients like CBD are helping people de-stress, but not everyone is looking to tune out or relieve anxiety."

"Aromatherapy provides an entire range of moods, from grounded to juicy and productive to visionary, and the seven chakras, when they are in tune, allow us to play beautiful energetic symphonies." She sees a return to clean and natural beauty as part of what she calls "conscious beauty," the return to a more meaningful way to share who we are not only on the outside but on the inside.

An aura reading and mood boost consultation with Laura and Jim is an experience you don't want to miss, because it's available in few stores anywhere. There is an authenticity at work here that makes it easy to sit down for a reading with this couple.

The store is filled with crystals, scents, and products specifically curated to remind you to adore yourself. The company blends and bottles its aromatherapy products in beautiful, custom, award-winning packaging that is a big part of the brand's appeal.

Aura readings are available at the Asheville store or at events when Jim and Laura travel to off-site locations, like this Valentine's Day, when they visited Canyon Ranch Spa in Tucson.

The ADORAtherapy line is available online at adoratherapy.com and in select spas like Canyon Ranch Tucson and specialty retailers.

We're grateful for our 100 5-star reviews. When our guests tell us how our products have worked for them, we know we're on the right track. In the store, we have incredible word-of-mouth and referrals. It's not uncommon for someone to bring their whole family and dog and then come back when the family is in town. We also love it when our guests post about it on social media. We can't get enough.

"Adoring ourselves is the hack we all need," says Laura. And anyone who believes they can get through their day without making their thoughts become things would be reminded to watch the movie *The Secret*. "It's not impossible to love ourselves. You just have to wake up every day and do it."

About the Author

Founder and Chief Mood Booster at ADORAtherapy, Laura is dedicated to reminding us to adore ourselves. Her award-winning aroma perfume brand allows her to bottle up her chakra healing wisdom so she can be the ultimate life coach in a bottle.

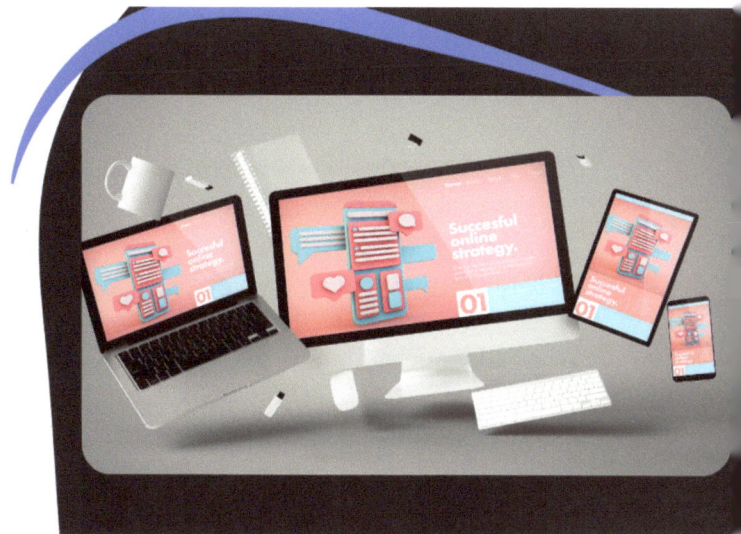

CHANGING THE WORLD WITH COMPASSION AND HUMANITY

SANDRA JACQUEMIN

We created this for everyone, and anyone who is passionate about changing the world for the better. Compassion is the only requirement here, which our subscribers are not short of. I believe that we do share one thing in common: *humanity*. It isn't always on the surface, but it is there. We've seen people jump to rescue someone in a burning car—no matter if they are straight, gay, black, white, Democrat or Republican, Christian, or Jewish—and I'm not trying to pigeonhole things. When someone hurts, the truth is we all hurt, we all feel it. I believe that at their core that most people don't want others to suffer. I believe we want the same things, joy, peace, happiness, and with that, there are so many individuals out there dedicating their time and lives to helping our world.

We go about our daily lives, sipping our Starbucks lattes, and moving about, not stopping to think about our thousands of soldiers in war zones. That hit home with my husband and realizing soon after what little to no support they get in the real world. This is so far beyond politics or beliefs, again, it is about humanity. I complain about not having A/C for a day because it broke down, and when you see a disabled grandmother taking care of her grandson in a shed, you stop. When you see there are people out there building homes with their bare hands and any materials they can get, crowdfunding to support others just because—*humanity*… you do something.

Starsoul is the *something* I decided to do.

Here's how I got here. Shortly after having my first son, watching the news and re-run episodes of Mom was what kept us up throughout the night while I was breastfeeding. All new parents know those long, endless nights. It felt like during that time, things took such a dark turn, 2019 became such a heavy year leading into 2020. The world felt heavy. Race and religion were under attack, equal rights were being challenged from every corner, political strife, and people tearing down one another. And there I was, holding a baby. We began to ask ourselves the most important question, *What were we really doing to make the world any better for him?* I had led some of the best marketing campaigns since 1998, introduced the first NBA and NFL franchise DJs, worked with race car drivers around the world, put together the most incredible events, even worked with Mickey Mouse.

But in the end, what would be left when we were gone? What would my son see? A black square I posted somewhere on my timeline years prior that I should pretend invoked any change? Or that I said, "Pray for the homeless" and poof—just like that? I didn't do any of that because I want my son to know, growing into this future digital world, that you can post and pray for change; you have to ACT ON IT. Yes, advocate by posting. Yes, have faith by praying. But put that into action.

All of that pushed me to do this, mid-pandemic, pulling together my resources and jumping in headfirst with our savings. With little to no budget, I decided I wanted to put people to work who were furloughed or needed work to help each other. I called a girlfriend from high school who is now a brilliant photographer, and while she had never photographed a large group like this, she was unbelievable and got us over eight hundred perfect shots in a couple of hours. An old colleague from years prior who designed one of my first business logos came through with his amazing talent to help us create our initial designs and other logos, including digitizing a heart we and our son drew together which would later become our February 2023 tee. Old high school friends showed up with friends and family to volunteer as our models.

Then, thinking we were ready to go with our first tees, concept, logo, plan, photo, year planned out, domain purchased, company registered—Shopify. That mountain was one I was not confident in climbing and we were ready to throw in the towel. We didn't have the budget to hire someone for thousands of dollars and decided maybe this was just not the time. In my mind, we were going to shelf this for another time. I randomly was watching an Instagram live and put my name in applying to win a Shopify build. And just when I was ready to give up, the Entreprenista League granted us the build. They were my angels and reason to push forward; it was sink or swim. I waited a week to tell my husband and said, "This is it, either we do it or bow out."

And with that, we dove in. On our first initial call with the team in NY, they asked when we wanted to launch. With no hesitation, we said, "December 10, Human Rights Day." They gasped because early October gave us less than three months to create the site.

But here we are.

What does Starsoul do? We created a new platform for giving, or as we like to say, a subscription to giving. Many causes affect many people in different ways. It is difficult to single out one thing that we care about over another. Sure, you can write a check to a charity and keep going, but this is so much more. With the t-shirts, we are not only raising funds, but helping people feel seen. The tees bring awareness and invoke thought at the same time. By dedicating one t-shirt to one cause per month, we can focus on more ways to support. We don't seek to just write a check to a charity. We connect with them, find out what their most immediate needs are, and most surprisingly, through this process we learn that it is not only awareness they seek but specific support for either an event or a mission.

For example, when we did Animal Rights month, it was very difficult to narrow it down. Dogs, dolphins, tigers—so many we wanted to help, but we didn't want to spread ourselves too thin. We decided we could always circle back to individual animals and humane societies, so we chose elephants, our son's favorite animal at the time. The first one he recognized at the zoo. So we connected with The Elephant Sanctuary in Tennessee, the largest in the country, and asked what their most immediate needs were and how we could help. They said the best way we could support them was by adopting an elephant—so we did. Choosing the elephant we wanted to adopt was easy. Because of our love for Disney, we adopted the elephant named Minnie.

When we connected with Lotus House shelter back in October for Domestic Violence and Anti-Bullying month, one of their most immediate needs was not only awareness for their mission but donations for their graduating tenants. One of their specific requests was for shoes for toddler boys. We were able to secure them over fifty pairs of brand-new sneakers from Reebok, a former client of mine, who stepped up to help and partner for future endeavors. We stayed committed well beyond October and have formed a bond with their amazing team, visiting them a couple of times a month. We've been able to donate new baby mattresses, clothing, housewares, electronics, toys, baby clothes, Halloween costumes for their annual party, and over $5,000 in donated items.

I've been in marketing since college where I decided to turn down agency jobs and open my own company while finishing up my last two years of my Bachelor's. I've had the privilege since then to work with clients like Reebok, HBO, Universal, Nickelodeon, and MTV for nearly two decades. We even promoted Justin Timberlake's first solo album. Time flies.

In 2014, in addition to continuing my work in marketing, I signed a contract with the one and only Walt Disney World to freelance with their broadcast and production teams. I've traveled the world working on different racetracks, learned from the very best at Disney, put together some of the most notable marketing campaigns and events, and yet none of it feels as significant as what we are accomplishing today.

My husband and I share one thing in common among many others: We are entrepreneurs at heart. He has built several successful businesses since his return from the Marines, and I knew we would make good partners in this venture. While I continue to work as a marketing consultant, the pandemic "shutdown" presented itself as an opportunity to create something that had a positive impact on the world. My husband and I put our heads (and savings) together and formulated a plan to conceptualize our idea for Starsoul, the first subscription that donates all proceeds to charities using t-shirts as the vehicle to raise funds and awareness for causes every month.

Spreading the word on what we do is the best way to help, besides subscribing, obviously. We get so many requests from people and charities and as we grow, we just want to help as many as we can. So many, just

want to be seen, and we see you! We celebrate and support you.

After the tragic hurricane Ian hit the west coast of Florida, a teacher reached out to us, devastated, and needing supplies. We had just highlighted education in August and had provided tons of supplies for kids in extreme poverty for the school year. Though September was Suicide Prevention month, we were able to send her much of what she needed from her Amazon list.

In parting, I would like to say this: You learn as you go. My mom always taught me to smile at the world. My father always said, "Never say no. Do it and figure out how to ride the horse later. You have this one life. It is an adventure, nothing is ever going to be perfect, and people will always judge you—so do it anyway!"

The best way for anyone to get involved or work with us is by emailing us at love@officialstarsoul.com or connecting with us via Instagram @officialstarsoul.

About the Author

Twenty years as a marketing leader, promoting some of the industry's greatest box office releases, sneakers, and beverages, introducing the NBA and NFL's first franchise DJs and taking on a male-dominated racing industry, Sandra continues her marketing consulting and launched the first charity t-shirt subscription over the pandemic, seeking to set an example for her son and change the world.

HELPING UNDERREPRESENTED COMMUNITIES ACHIEVE NATURAL WELLNESS

NAILAH QUEEN

Our goal is to help people who live in underrepresented communities and may not have access to education and awareness about healthy lifestyles to prevent disease and promote natural living. Our ideal clients are those who want to change their lives by gaining access to healthy options and knowledge. Our goal is to change the picture so that people in these communities don't have to wait until they're diagnosed to learn about prevention and treatment options.

We promote healthy wellness alternatives to underrepresented communities by raising awareness and introducing convenient, easy-to-use products that can be integrated into everyday life without interruption. Our product line is tailored to address the most common health issues in the African American community, including diabetes, hypertension, obesity, anxiety, and arthritis. Our goal is to provide affordable and effective solutions for the entire family.

We take great pride in offering hair and body care products that are made from 100% natural ingredients. This is a differentiator that is rare in natural health and beauty, but highly valued by our customers. Unlike many products in the market that contain synthetic additives, our organic formulas are gentle, safe, and nourishing for skin and hair.

Our commitment to using only natural ingredients applies to all of our products, including hair care, skin care and body care. We handpick our ingredients and choose only the best and most beneficial botanicals and natural oils for our formulas. This allows us to offer our customers products that aren't only effective, but also safe for everyday use.

Our hair care line is characterized primarily by the use of natural and organic ingredients. We know that hair care can be a difficult balance between achieving the desired look and maintaining healthy hair. Our products are made with natural ingredients that gently cleanse, moisturize, and nourish hair without harsh chemicals that can strip hair of its natural oils or damage it.

We believe it's a great advantage for our brand that it's completely "natural" and doesn't contain "special ingredients" that are difficult to pronounce. We know consumers are becoming more and more concerned about using natural products for their beauty care and are looking for transparency in ingredient lists. We make it easy for our customers to know exactly what they're putting on their hair and skin, and we're committed to providing them with the best possible natural products.

After experiencing the stress of the pandemic, I noticed my hair was falling out and my body was struggling to recover from the effects of COVID-19. Determined to find a solution, I set out to develop hair and body care products that would provide the protection and nutrients I needed. The results were remarkable, and I knew I had to share these products with others who were struggling with similar issues. And so Regally Insane was born.

What started as a personal mission to restore my hair and body health has become a way for me to give back to my community, especially African Americans who rarely have access to healthy options, from nutrition to medical care. I believe everyone deserves to have access to products that promote wellness, and I'm committed to making that a reality with Regally Insane.

Our products are made from natural and organic ingredients that provide the necessary nutrients and protection for healthy hair and a healthy body. We pride ourselves on offering alternatives and helpful products that are tailored to our customers' individual needs. Our brand has allowed me to change not only my own life, but the lives of the people I serve.

We want to give back to our community by partnering with other small businesses and taking part in community outreach programs. By doing so, we hope to have a positive impact on the lives of those around us. At Regally Insane, we believe everyone deserves to feel confident and empowered in their own skin, and we're committed to making that a reality for everyone.

The inspiration for my business came from my late mother, who always encouraged me to pursue my passions and find something I love to do. She instilled in me the belief that if you find something you love, you'll excel at it and make a positive impact on the world. In this way, she wanted to help me live a full life and leave a lasting legacy for my family.

Following her advice, I started my business with a deep sense of purpose and commitment. I wanted to create a brand that not only reflected my passion but also embodied the values my mother instilled in me. Her wise words have proven true, and my love for what I do is the driving force behind my success.

My business is more than just a way to earn a living; it's a way for me to give back to my community and improve the lives of others. I'm proud to carry on my mother's legacy

through my work and honor her memory in everything I do.

I believe everyone has a unique gift or talent to share with the world. It's up to each of us to find what we love to do and use that passion to make a positive difference. For me, that means building a business that reflects my values and embodies my mother's spirit. I hope my story inspires others to follow their own passions and create a legacy they can be proud of.

You can find us online at RegallyInsane.com as well as on social media through Facebook, Instagram, Twitter, and TikTok under the handle @RegallyInsane. We are also available via email for those who may have questions at askus@regallyinsane.com

Please share a post or tag the business @ regally insane in all posts or platforms on social media or by word of mouth.

About the Author

I'm Nailah Queen, wife, mother, CEO, philanthropist, innovator, self-care advocate, business mentor, influencer, travel enthusiast, and serial entrepreneur. It's important to be part of the change we want to see, and entrepreneurship allows us to have a seat at the table without having to ask for it.

EXPERT ADVICE FOR STARTING AND SUSTAINING A SUCCESSFUL HOME CARE BUSINESS

JULIA AKINYOOYE

My ideal clients are those interested in starting or growing their home care business. These include aspiring entrepreneurs, new business owners, and established businesses. They're people who want to comply with government regulations, grow their business and expand their agency.

These clients are business-minded, motivated, and innovative healthcare leaders. They aren't interested in just doing the bare minimum, but want to develop strategic programs, measure outcomes, and improve the patient experience. They want to transform the home care industry and believe in making it more humane.

For these ideal clients, it's important to not just provide basic care, but to truly understand their patients' needs and develop an individualized care plan. They want to provide quality care that allows patients to remain in their own homes and still receive the medical care they need. They understand the importance of compassionate care and how it can positively affect the lives of their patients and their families.

There are two main issues that home care entrepreneurs face with compliance. One is getting state licensure for home care and the other is complying with state standards while operating.

At Emmanuel Consulting Agency, we offer comprehensive consulting services. We assist with obtaining state licensure and provide training, mentorship, and preparation to help companies comply with regulations and further improve patient outcomes.

We provide training and mentoring in the form of one-on-one coaching, formalized training programs specifically for executives, and conduct mock surveys. This helps our clients understand what they need to grow and expand their businesses, comply with regulations, and limit legal liabilities. It also helps our clients deliver a high-quality program for better patient care.

At Emmanuel Consulting Agency, we offer a range of consulting services. One of our most important services is assisting clients in applying for a home care license in the state of their choice. We have a 100% success rate in obtaining such a license. We also offer a customized training program for our home care executives that is mandatory when you sign up with us. It has been our experience that clients who receive training prior to starting their business perform better and have a greater impact on the communities in which they serve.

As a clinician and trained nurse in nursing education, I'm passionate about providing customized training. I believe everyone learns differently and that the responsibility of running a home care business and caring for a vulnerable population requires extensive training. That is why I offer small workshops for home care providers, showing them how to deal with the problems of the industry.

Besides our licensing and training services, we also help create and update policies and procedures to ensure compliance, and we can assist with agency purchases and sales if the client desires. Our agency is committed to providing value and innovation to our clients. That's why this spring, for the first time, I'm hosting a roundtable conference called "The DPS Conference" specifically for NY LHCSA to educate patient service leaders on compliance measures, value-based care, regulatory requirements, and how to deal with staffing shortages.

Our startup package and mock surveys are among our most popular offerings. The startup package provides our clients with the foundation they need to run and grow their business, giving them the confidence they need. Our clients are mentored throughout the startup process and receive a comprehensive training program, including our NY LHCSA Training Program for Nurses and Administrators TM, designed by industry experts specifically to meet the needs of home care executives. This program is included in our home care startup consulting package.

We also offer mock surveys to help companies comply with state standards. Our team conducts a comprehensive survey of the business, identifies areas that need improvement, and provides detailed feedback on how to address these issues. Our goal is to help our clients limit legal liability, improve patient outcomes, and provide quality patient care programs.

At Emmanuel Consulting Agency, we provide customized solutions to our clients. We understand that each organization has its own needs and challenges, and we tailor our services accordingly. We provide our clients with the support and guidance they need to succeed in the home care industry.

We offer a mentorship program that includes access to our Preferred Vendor Network to help clients run and scale their business. Our network is made up of reputable vendors, and we pass these benefits on to our clients to make it easier and more cost-effective for them. We also offer a survey service that mimics surveys conducted by government agencies. This helps our clients understand government expectations, prepare for the surveys, and run their business with confidence.

For companies that aren't our clients and are audited, we develop a realistic and concrete plan for their business. Our nurse consultants work with agency owners and executives to develop the plan and submit it to regulatory agencies. We provide project management to implement the corrective action plan within specific deadlines to avoid duplicate citations, fines, or closure. We also assist with facility reassessment to ensure the plan has been fully implemented and is 100% compliant by the target date.

At Emmanuel Consulting Agency, we provide solutions for established companies to maintain compliance. One of our services is the NY LHCSA Annual Compliance Subscription, a subscription-based program for new and experienced NY LHCSAs who want to ensure they're in compliance with NY DOH policies and procedures, quality assurance program requirements, and emergency preparedness plans. Our team works closely with clients to meet annual compliance requirements and give them the peace of mind they need to focus on patient care.

Clients who comply with our program typically have better patient outcomes, higher employee retention, and are more profitable. They also perform well in re-licensure audits. We know that compliance can be a daunting task. That's why we strive to make it as easy and stress-free as possible for our customers.

As a certified accreditation consultant with ACHC, I help home care agencies get accreditation for their home health, hospice, and private duty nursing services.

Accreditation is a process by which healthcare organizations show they meet national standards. With accreditation, these organizations show they meet high standards that ensure better performance and patient care. Accreditation provides home care agencies with many benefits, including a competitive advantage, a strong reputation, opportunities for expansion, and improved performance metrics. It helps provide structure, strengthens the organization's brand, and facilitates the delivery of quality-based services.

Though I am an ACHC-certified consultant my team and I do provide all readiness prep for all accrediting bodies to get your home care agency accredited including CAHC Commission on Accreditation Home Care, Inc. Community Health Accreditation Partner CHAP, The Joint Commission, and the National Institute for Home care Accreditation.

Our agency provides brokerage services for those looking to buy or sell a home care agency. When selling an agency, we help locate potential buyers and advise them on industry trends, strengths, and weaknesses, and perform due diligence. We help our clients prepare their agency for sale at least three years in advance to maximize profit.

To ensure a smooth transition, we help agencies understand specific industry regulations and the duties of the new owner. We also work to increase the value of services provided, improve key performance indicators, increase revenue, and address compliance issues or plan of corrections. In addition, we assist with the proper transfer of ownership.

On the buy side, we locate potential home care agencies for sale and perform due diligence by preparing questions for the seller and analyzing reports to understand agency functionality, current and past liabilities, and compliance issues. Our goal is to provide comprehensive services to assist in the purchase or sale of a home care agency.

Emmanuel Consulting Agency was founded after I was recommended to a gentleman who wanted to start his home care business in New York. Since I was already working in the industry as a registered nurse with experience in community health care, case management, and home care directorship, I was confident that I could help him get licensure and provide comprehensive consulting services. After he passed inspection and successfully launched his business, I realized there was a gap in the industry in terms of understanding the processes, importance, and compliance required to start and maintain a home care business. This prompted me to provide consulting services to more clients.

I want to tell you a success story about a single mother who dreamed of starting her own home care business. She was so determined to make her dream a reality that she took out a second mortgage to finance it. Unfortunately, the consulting agency she hired out of state could not help her successfully run her business or get licensed. As a result, she turned to us at Emmanuel Consulting Agency. We not only helped her get the necessary license, but also mentored her throughout the startup process. Now, just two years later, she's done nearly $2 million in sales. We're incredibly proud of her and her hard work and dedication. She has earned a reputation for taking care of hard-to-serve patients in areas where access to services is limited.

So the best way to work with us is to have a phone conversation. In this conversation, we get a full picture of what you want and explain who we're, our accomplishments, our services, and our mission. We'll set clear expectations for working together, and if there's a good opportunity to work together, we'll put a plan in place to make it happen.

The best way to share our work is word of mouth and talking about your experience with our company. Feedback in the form of reviews and testimonials from customers is greatly appreciated. They help others learn about our company and the home care solutions we provide. When our clients leave reviews, other potential clients know what to expect from our consulting firm, and they feel confident in choosing us as their consulting firm. It also lets us know how we're serving them and what we can do to improve our services.

One piece of advice I can give to clients or potential clients who want to get into home care is to do your research. It's important that you have a clear mission, vision and goal when starting a home care business. Make sure you have the necessary resources, whether financial, training or mentors, to sustain this type of business, which is highly regulated and can be profitable, but also requires a lot of work, paperwork, compliance with regulations, policies, procedures

and dealing with the sick and the public. If you want to serve, this is for you, but if you're all about profit, it's not for you.

I recommend you have support, time, and financial backing because coordinating services like home care can be stressful, and you may be dealing with professionals and paraprofessionals who don't always see eye to eye. By sharpening your leadership, problem-solving and customer service skills, you can avoid or minimize pitfalls and maintain good employees and a positive work culture. It's important that you have a professional support system that includes other business owners, mentors, consultants, attorneys, and accountants who can advise you on day-to-day issues. It's also important that you keep up with the latest regulations and technology in home care because technology can make your business more efficient, but don't forget the human approach, which can't be replaced.

About the Author

Julia Akinyooye is a league member and CEO of Emmanuel Consulting Agency, a home care business consulting firm based in NY. She helps home care businesses obtain licensure, grow, and run their business in compliance so they have peace of mind.

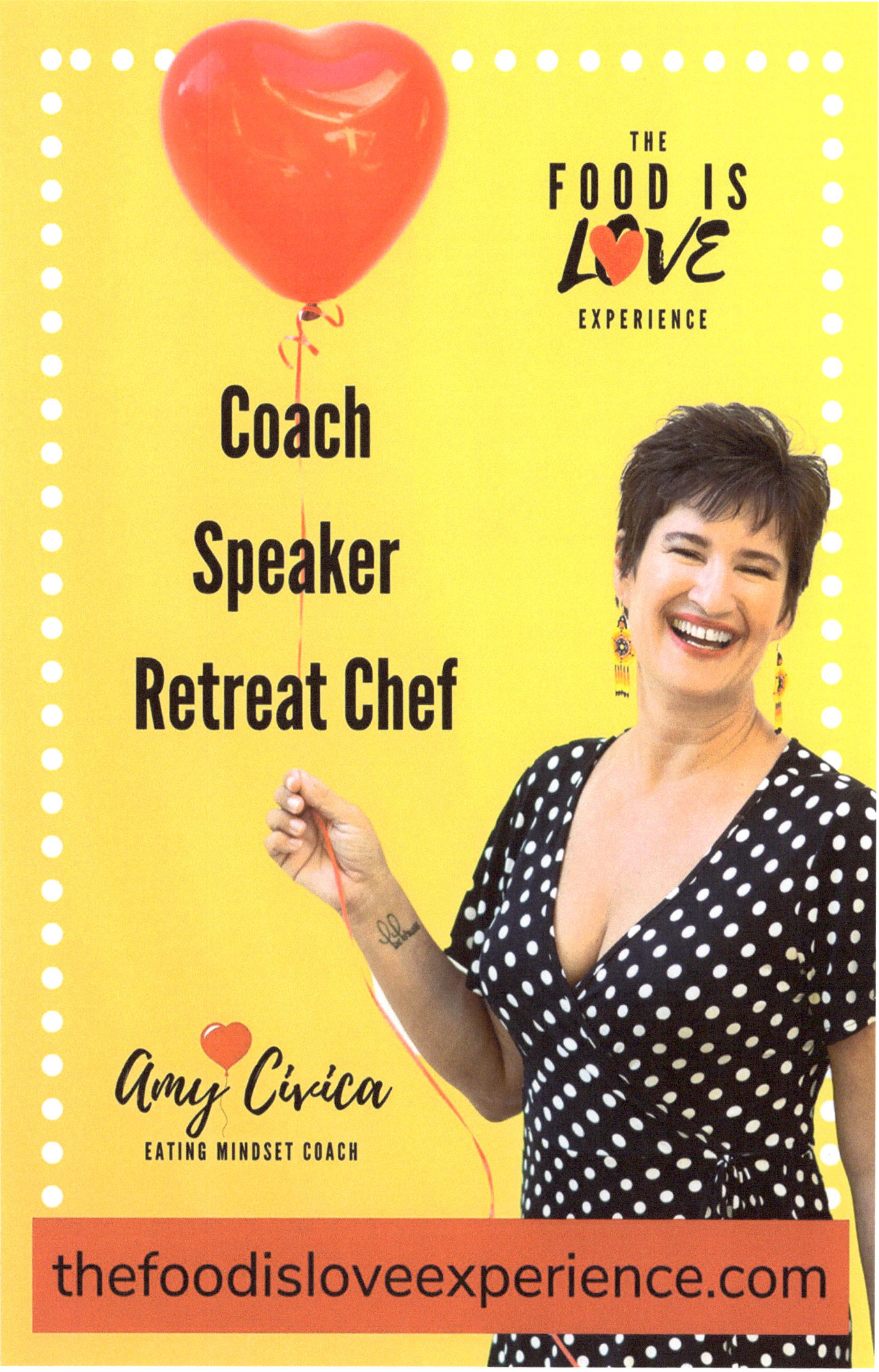
THE
FOOD IS
LOVE
EXPERIENCE
Coach
Speaker
Retreat Chef
Amy Civica
EATING MINDSET COACH
thefoodisloveexperience.com

ADVERTISERS

www.ingramcontent.com/pod-product-compliance
Lightning Source LLC
Chambersburg PA
CBHW041452210326
41599CB00004B/228